WHAT IS ART?

Buildings

KAREN HOSACK

CHICAGO, ILLINOIS

Customer Service 888-454-2279
Visit our website at www.heinemannraintree.com

Editorial: Adam Miller, Charlotte Guillain, Clare Lewis,
and Catherine Veitch
Design: Victoria Bevan and AMR Design Ltd
Illustrations: David Woodroffe
Picture Research: Mica Brancic
and Helen Reilly/Arnos Design Ltd
Production: Victoria Fitzgerald

Originated by Modern Age
Printed and bound by CTPS (China Translation and
Printing Services Ltd)

13 12 11 10 09
10 9 8 7 6 5 4 3 2 1

Library of Congress Cataloging-in-Publication Data
Hosack, Karen.
  Buildings / Karen Hosack.
    p. cm. -- (What is art?)
  Includes bibliographical references and index.
  ISBN 978-1-4109-3165-8 (hc)
  1. Buildings--Juvenile literature. 2. Architecture--
Juvenile literature. I. Title.
  NA2555.H67 2008
  720--dc22
                                    2008009700

Acknowledgments
The publishers would like to thank the following for
permission to reproduce photographs:
©Alamy pp. **5** (Ian Dagnall), **11** (Travelshots.com),
19 (PCL), **22** (Images Etc Ltd), **24** (Peter Barritt);
©Corbis pp. **4** (Christophe Boisvieux), **7** (Richard
Cooke), **8** (Arcaid), **18** (Danny Lehman), **26** (Rudy
Sulgan); ©Dreamstime p. **21**; ©Getty pp. **9** (Axiom
Photographic Agency), **13** (Romilly Lockyer), **15** (Tim
Boyle), **27** (Stone+/Stephen Schauer); ©istockphoto
pp. **6** (fotoVoyager), **10** (David Iliff), **14** (H Peter
Weber), **20** (Lawrence Freytag), **23** (Klaas Lingbeek-
van Kranen); ©Rex Features pp. **12** (Andrew Drysdale),
16 (Eye Ubiquitous), **17** (Stock Connection/Cosmo
Condina); ©2008 Banco de México Diego Rivera &
Frida Kahlo Museums Trust. Av. Cinco de Mayo No.2,
Col. Centro, Del. Cuauhtémoc 06059, México, D.F0
Scala Art Library p. **25**.

Cover photograph of Atrium of Santiago Grand Hyatt
Hotel, Santiago, Chile, reproduced with permission of
Corbis/Richard T. Nowitz.

Every effort has been made to contact copyright
holders of any material reproduced in this book.
Any omissions will be rectified in subsequent
printings if notice is given to the publishers.

Contents

Any words appearing in the text in bold, **like this**, are explained in the glossary.

Looking at Buildings

People plan and construct buildings for many reasons. People live, worship, go to events, and work in buildings. Buildings are places where people come together. How buildings look can often give us a clue about what they are used for.

Religion

This building is used by people who follow the religion of Buddhism. This religion started in India in the 6th century BCE. Most Japanese towns and cities have Buddhist temples, which often include a main hall, like this one, a gateway, and a cemetery where people are buried.

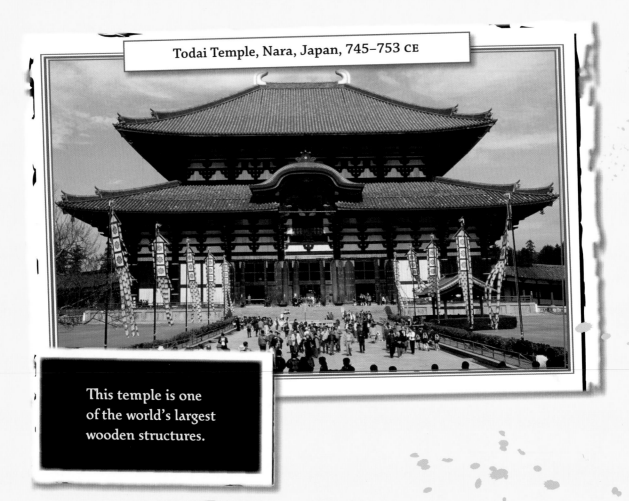

Todai Temple, Nara, Japan, 745–753 CE

This temple is one of the world's largest wooden structures.

As a place for showing exhibitions, why do you think this building needs large spaces?

Did you know?
"Architecture" is the word we give to different styles and types of buildings. Architects are people who design buildings.

Pompidou Center, Paris, France, 1972–76

Art

The Pompidou Center in Paris, France, is an amazing building with many large glass windows that allow the viewer to see almost all the way through it. It was **designed** as a museum and art gallery. One problem the **architect** had was where to hide the pipes for the air conditioning and water supply. He solved the problem by making them part of the building's design and painting the pipes in bright colors.

Homes

Architects designed both of these buildings as homes. What do they say about the people who live in them?

Palaces and castles

Buckingham Palace is the official home of the queen of England and her family. It has been the London home of British kings and queens since 1837. The royal family uses many of its 600 rooms for special events, such as banquets for leaders of other countries. These rooms contain antique furniture and many famous works of art, and some areas are open to the public as a museum.

Buckingham Palace, London, 1705

Would you like having your home opened up to the public?

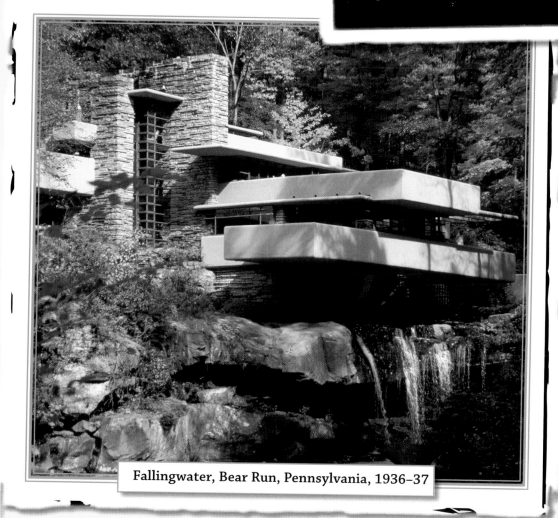

Fallingwater, Bear Run, Pennsylvania, 1936–37

Natural surroundings

The U.S. architect Frank Lloyd Wright believed that the buildings he designed should fit in with nature. He thought this would affect the way people lived their lives. This is one of the architect's most famous designs for a private home. You can see how it is surrounded by trees and how the waterfall seems to come from the building.

Think about it!
Think about your own home. What makes it different from public buildings, such as schools, libraries, or stores?

Ideas from Nature

The **architects** who **designed** the two buildings shown here also got ideas from the natural world.

Trees or bones?

The Spanish architect Antoni Gaudí designed very unusual buildings. Many of them are in Barcelona, Spain. They seem to grow from the ground, with their curved edges and tree-like structures, although most are made from **concrete**. There are very few straight lines, and one side of a building does not always match the other. This is called **organic** architecture.

Casa Batllo, Barcelona, Spain, 1904–6

People in Barcelona call this building the "House of Bones" because they think the columns look like bones. Other people think they look like elephants' legs.

Bird or fish?

The Milwaukee Art Museum is on the banks of Lake Michigan, in Wisconsin. The building includes a giant sunscreen that opens out like wings when the museum is open. It looks a bit like a giant bird sitting at the side of the lake. The wings even flap each day at noon to entertain visitors.

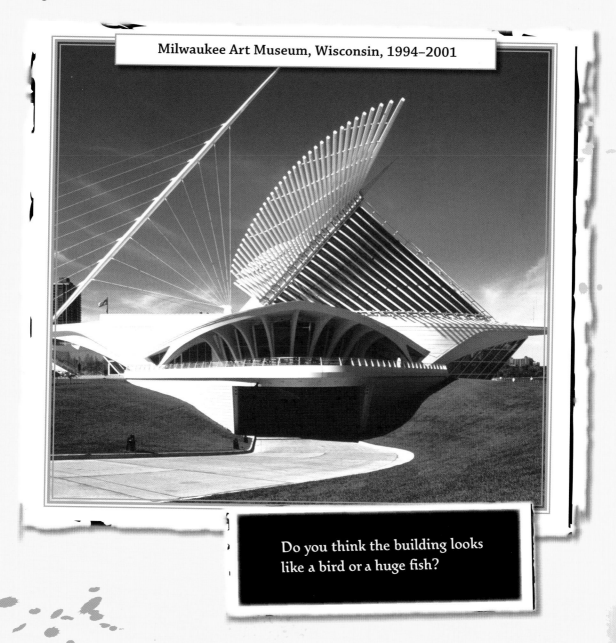

Milwaukee Art Museum, Wisconsin, 1994–2001

Do you think the building looks like a bird or a huge fish?

Large Public Spaces

The Colosseum is a large building in Rome, Italy, that was finished in 82 CE. It is called an **amphitheater**, and up to 50,000 people could sit inside. It was used for large public events such as gladiator fights, executions, and plays. Its round shape, with the stage in the center, meant that everyone had a good view of the action.

Did you know?
Today, the Colosseum is partly ruined because of earthquakes and people taking the stones. But it is still a very popular tourist attraction and a reminder of Rome's ancient history.

Many people would gather in the Colosseum to be entertained.

The Colosseum, Rome, Italy, 70–82 CE

This theater, called the Globe, was designed in a similar way to the Colosseum. The audience is closer to the drama because the stage is in the center of the building. The first Globe was built from wood and **thatch** in London in 1599, and many of Shakespeare's plays were performed there. In 1613 an accidental fire caused it to burn down. A second building was built in the same place before Shakespeare died, but it was closed and knocked down in 1644.

The Globe, London, 1997

This photograph shows the new Globe Theater, which was built near the site of the old Globe. It was opened in 1997.

Celebrating an Age

Some buildings are **designed** to celebrate their time in history. The **Industrial Revolution** was a time of great change in the world. One of these changes was the invention of the steam railroad. People were looking to the future with hope and excitement. Building a station was therefore a very good way to show this feeling of celebration. Paddington Station in London has a beautiful arched roof made of glass and wrought iron. Viewers get an idea of the wealth at the time from this heavily decorated roof and the stone figures around the front entrance.

Paddington Station was designed by Isambard Kingdom Brunel, who also designed many other buildings, bridges, and tunnels in the 19th century.

Paddington Station, London, 1852–54

Biggest and best?

In the 1920s there was competition among **architects** to produce the tallest building in the world. The Eiffel Tower in Paris was the tallest structure for some time, but the Chrysler Building in New York City overtook it in 1930. The building was the dream of the car manufacturer Walter P. Chrysler. It did not keep the title of tallest building for long. One year after it was finished, the Empire State Building was built.

At the top of the Chrysler Building, there are **gargoyles** in the shape of car ornaments.

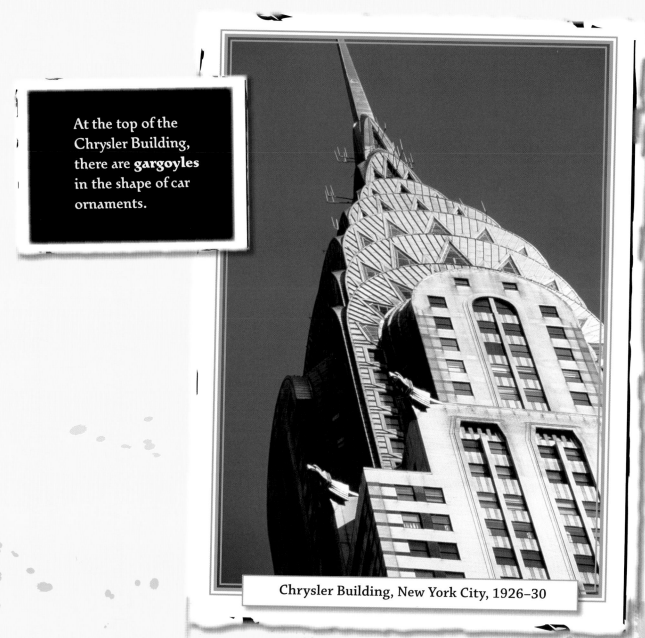

Chrysler Building, New York City, 1926–30

Materials

The Chrysler Building was mainly made from metal. Today, people are starting to use more natural materials that are better for the environment. In Scandinavia, people have been living in wooden buildings for a long time. The wood is specially treated so that moisture cannot damage the house. The trees come from **sustainable** forests, and less energy is used to produce "green buildings" (see below).

Log home, Scandinavia

Wooden houses that are made of trees from sustainable forests are known as "green buildings."

Green roofs

For centuries people have used natural materials to **insulate** their homes. **Thatched** roofs were very popular, but fire could easily damage them. Today, some people use the natural warmth of soil and grass on the roof to protect a building. It is important that the roof is waterproof and that water can drain away well.

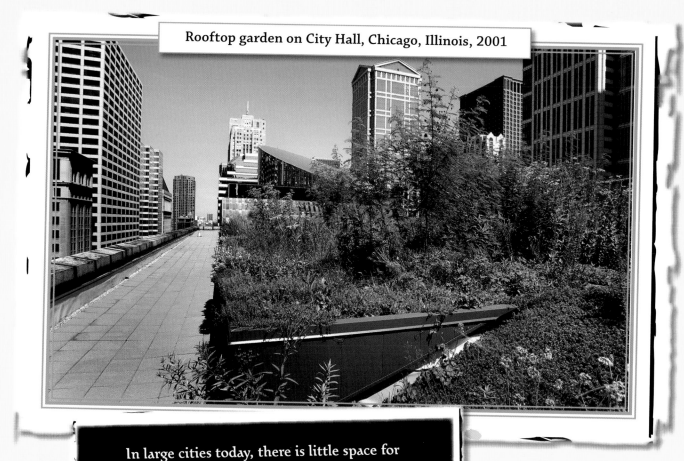

Rooftop garden on City Hall, Chicago, Illinois, 2001

In large cities today, there is little space for gardens or parks. Some people like to turn their roofs into green spaces.

Old and New

This strange-looking building is known as the "Gherkin," a British word for "pickle." Can you see why? This modern building is close to the historic center of London, where there are many old and famous buildings. It was **designed** to be as good for the environment as possible. The huge glass windows bring a large amount of daylight into the building, so people do not need to turn on lights. Air is brought into the building in natural ways so that the people who work there do not always use air-conditioning.

How do you think people reacted to this structure when it was being built?

Swiss Re Tower, London, England, 2001–2004

What do you think about this very modern building sitting next to the old museum?

Think about it!
Some people believe that any new buildings constructed next to old buildings should match in style and materials. Other people think it is more interesting to show something new and different. What do you think?

The Louvre pyramid, Paris, France, 1989

Does it fit?

The Louvre is a very famous art museum in Paris. In 1989 a modern glass pyramid was added to the much-loved building. Many people could not understand how a structure so different in shape and materials could sit alongside the much older museum. However, over time people have started to like the new building and think that it celebrates their own age.

Cities and Their Buildings

Large cities are often built around rivers or on the coast. This is because water used to be the fastest way to move materials and people.

Venice

The city of Venice, Italy, is spread over a number of islands that are joined together by canals. Many of the beautiful buildings that survive today were built in the time of the **Renaissance**, when many artists and designers lived in Venice. Light reflects off the water in the canals onto the light stone and marble architecture.

Today, pollution and damage to the foundations of the city are big problems in Venice.

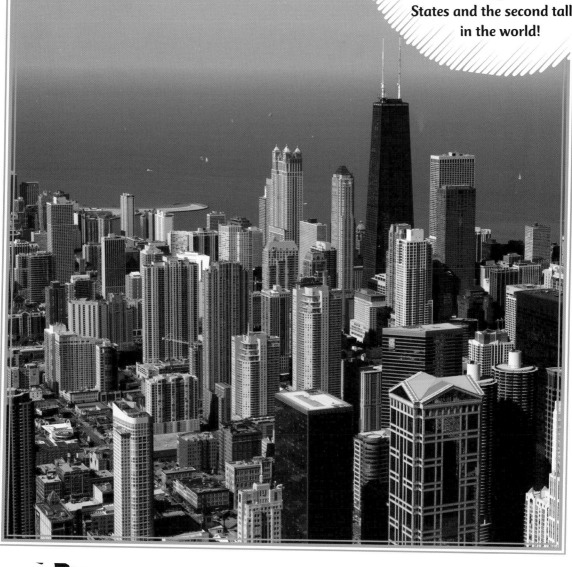

The Chicago **skyline** is much more modern than Venice. It also grew up next to water, in this case Lake Michigan. The lake is now reflected in many of the numerous skyscrapers that show the city's success and wealth.

Places of Power

The Capitol, in Washington, D.C., looks very impressive with its large dome. Work began on it in 1793. The Capitol has two large wings on either side of the dome. One is for the House of Representatives, the other is for the Senate. These two groups make up **Congress**. Congress is responsible for making the laws in the United States.

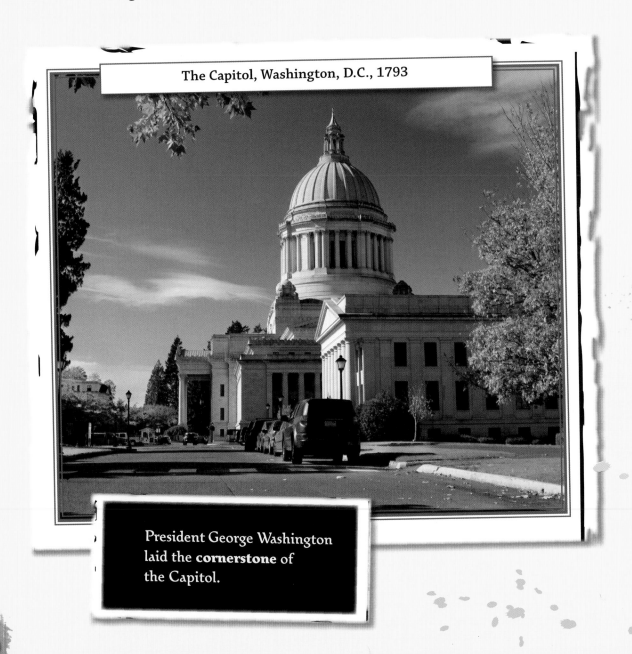

The Capitol, Washington, D.C., 1793

President George Washington laid the **cornerstone** of the Capitol.

The large clock tower on the side of the building is known as Big Ben. It is named after the bell inside the tower.

The Houses of Parliament, London, England, 1870

The Houses of **Parliament** in London are famous all over the world. Governments have ruled from this place for over 1,000 years. This building was finished in 1870. It is home to the British government and serves the same purpose as the Capitol building in the United States.

Symbolic building

The White House is the official home of the president of the United States. When people see an image of the White House on television, they know that the report is about the U.S. government and not about the building itself.

Memorials

Some buildings are made to remember a person. They remind viewers about an individual's achievements or how much the person was loved by those left behind.

The Taj Mahal in India was built by Emperor Shah Jahan in memory of his wife. The massive white marble building was constructed between 1632 and 1647. The craftsmanship is amazing, especially because it was done without the help of modern technology. The beautiful balance of the building is reflected in the water at the front, making it look as though it is floating.

Taj Mahal, Agra, India, 1632–47

How do you think the emperor felt about his wife?

Do you think Lincoln would have been pleased with his memorial?

Did you know?

Abraham Lincoln is famous for keeping the United States together during the Civil War (1861–65). He was shot and killed in 1865, shortly after the war ended.

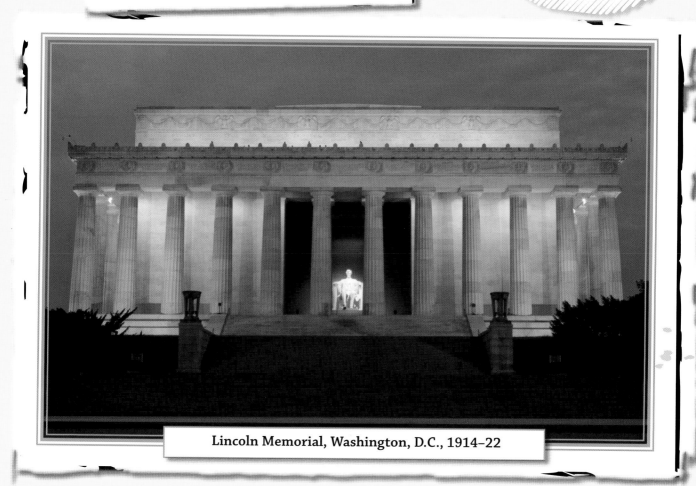

Lincoln Memorial, Washington, D.C., 1914–22

Public memory

This memorial was built in memory of the 16th president of the United States, Abraham Lincoln. The building is made up of 36 columns, one column for each U.S. state at the time. Inside, there is a 19-foot- (6-meter-) high sculpture of Lincoln sitting and thinking. The site of the memorial is now used for many large public gatherings and **political** protests.

On the Inside

The inside of a building can be as interesting as the outside. Buildings can come to life when there is decoration on the walls, floors, and ceilings.

This Italian **Renaissance** ceiling painting was started in 1508 and finished in 1512. It is painted on plaster using a technique called **fresco**. The plaster had to be damp so that it did not absorb the oil paint too much. This meant the artist and his assistants needed to work very quickly. Once you know this, the painting becomes even more impressive.

The Sistine Chapel, Rome, Italy, 1512

You can see this ceiling in the Sistine Chapel in Rome. It is part of the official residence of the pope, the Roman Catholic leader.

What does this mural tell us about how people spent their leisure time? What clothes did they wear to go to the park?

Dream of a Sunday Afternoon in the Alameda Park by Diego Rivera, 1947–48

During the Great Depression in the 1930s, people in the United States began painting frescoes. Artists were given money to set up projects by the Works Progress Administration (known as the WPA). Many thousands of workers took part to show what ordinary Americans were feeling, and the frescoes were put in places where many people would gather. These **murals** tell us about what was important to people at the time.

Buildings All Around Us

In this book we have looked at many reasons why people **design** and construct buildings. We have also looked at different materials that **architects** use and how buildings can represent a variety of things.

Buildings are part of our everyday life. It is very easy to just walk past them without thinking too much about why they are there and who might have designed them.

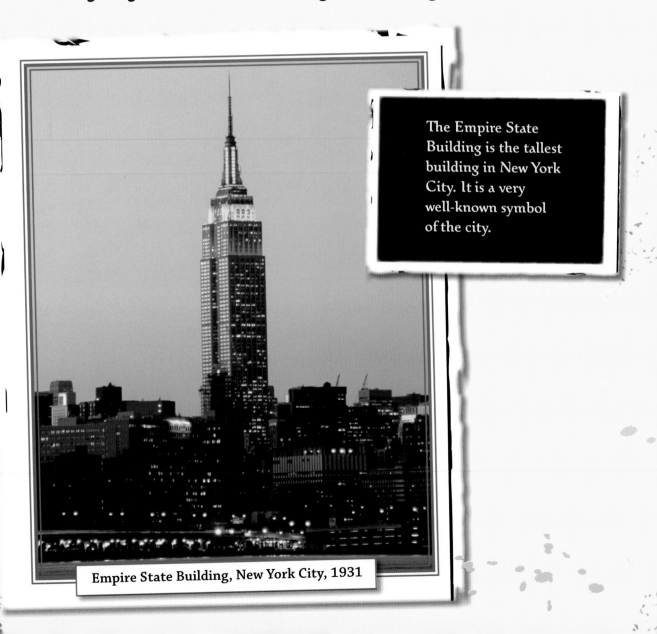

The Empire State Building is the tallest building in New York City. It is a very well-known symbol of the city.

Empire State Building, New York City, 1931

Clapboard home, California

Buildings become very familiar to us and can actually make us feel "at home." You might think about a landmark near where you live as being "home." You probably think that the building you live in with your family is the place you belong. We really can become attached to the buildings around us.

Timeline

82 CE	The Colosseum, Rome, Italy (p. 10)
745–753	Todai Temple, Nara, Japan (p. 4)
1097	The walls of the Houses of Parliament, London, England, first built and then extensively added to over the next centuries (p. 21)
1512	The Sistine Chapel ceiling, Vatican, Rome, Italy, by Michelangelo (p. 24)
1599	Shakespeare's Globe, London, England (rebuilt, 1997) (p. 11)
1632–1647	Taj Mahal, India (p. 22)
1705	Buckingham Palace, London, England (p. 6)
1793	The Capitol, Washington, D.C. (p. 20)
1852–1854	Paddington Station, London, England (p. 12)
1904–1906	Casa Batllo, Barcelona, Spain, **designed** by Antoni Gaudí (p. 8)
1914–1922	Lincoln Memorial, Washington, D.C., designed by Henry Bacon (p. 23)
1926–1930	Chrysler Building, New York City, designed by William Van Alen (p. 13)
1931	Empire State Building, New York City, designed by William Lamb (p. 26)
1936–1937	Fallingwater, Bear Run, Pennsylvania, designed by Frank Lloyd Wright (p. 7)
1947–1948	*Dream of a Sunday Afternoon in the Alameda Park* by Diego Rivera (p. 25)
1972–1976	Pompidou Center, Paris, France, designed by Richard Rogers and Renzo Piano (p. 5)
1989	The Louvre pyramid, Paris, France, designed by I. M. Pei (p. 17)
1994–2001	Milwaukee Art Museum, Wisconsin, designed by Santiago Calatrava (p. 9)
2001	Rooftop garden, City Hall, Chicago, Illinois (p. 15)
2001–2004	Swiss Re Tower, London, England, designed by Norman Foster (p. 16)

Where to See Buildings

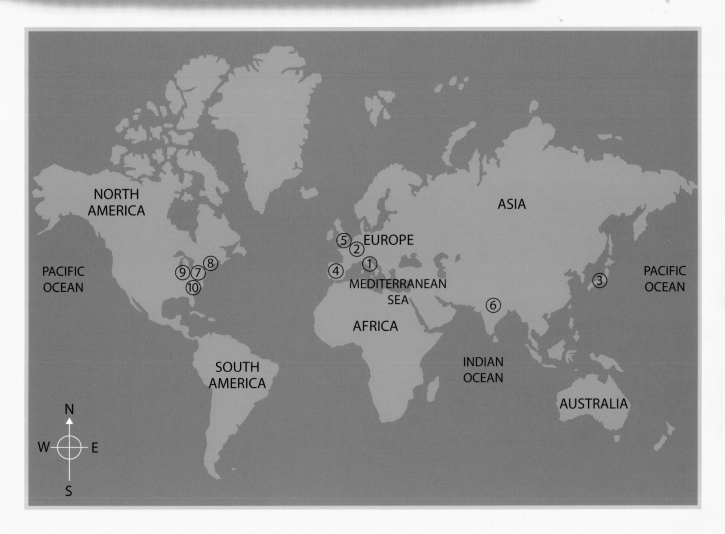

This map shows where you can see some of the buildings in this book.

1. **Rome, Italy**
   The Sistine Chapel
   The Colosseum
2. **Paris, France**
   Pompidou Center
   The Louvre pyramid
3. **Nara, Japan**
   Todai Temple
4. **Barcelona, Spain**
   Casa Batllo

5. **London, England**
   The Houses of
     Parliament
   Shakespeare's Globe
   Buckingham Palace
   Paddington Station
   Swiss Re Tower
6. **India**
   Taj Mahal

7. **Washington, D.C.**
   The White House
   Lincoln Memorial
   Capitol building
8. **New York City**
   Chrysler Building
   Empire State Building
9. **Chicago, Illinois**
   City Hall
10. **Bear Run, Pennsylvania**
   Fallingwater

Glossary

amphitheater circular building with no roof and with rows of seating

architect person who designs buildings

concrete mixture of sand, cement, and water used in building

Congress group of people, made up of the Senate and House of Representatives, that meets in the Capitol building and makes laws for the United States

cornerstone first stone laid down when a building is built

design plan and draw pictures of how something will look

fresco painting that is made on damp plaster

gargoyle face or figure in the roof of a building, sometimes forming a spout from a gutter

Industrial Revolution period of time in the 19th century when more machinery and factories began to be used

insulate use some sort of material to keep heat inside a building or other object

mural picture painted directly onto a wall

organic how plants and animals grow naturally

Parliament group of people who make the laws of the United Kingdom

political interest in how countries are governed

Renaissance period of European history between the 14th and 16th centuries when there was a renewed interest in art

skyline outline of hills and buildings

sustainable to ensure a future

thatch roofing made of straw or reeds

Learn More

Books to read

Goodman, Susan E. *Skyscraper: From the Ground Up*. New York: Knopf, 2004.

Oxlade, Chris. *Building Amazing Structures: Skyscrapers*. Chicago: Heinemann Library, 2006.

Oxlade, Chris. *Building Amazing Structures: Stadiums*. Chicago: Heinemann Library, 2006.

Royston, Angela. *Eco-Action: Buildings of the Future*. Chicago: Heinemann Library, 2008.

Websites to visit

Visit the official Empire State Building website. There is a section just for kids.

www.esbnyc.com

Explore the Taj Mahal and learn all about its past.

www.tajmahal.org.uk

Discover the work of many great architects.

www.greatbuildings.com/architects

Index